Collins

easy learning

Handwriting

Ages 5–7

How to use this book

- Find a quiet, comfortable place to work, away from distractions.

- Tackle one topic at a time.

- Help with reading the instructions where necessary and ensure that your child understands what to do.

- If your child is left-handed, check with your child's school to find out how they teach letter formation; some of the strokes will be made in the opposite direction to right-handed writers.

- The National Curriculum states that children should be taught to understand which letters, when next to one another, are best left unjoined. These are called break letters. Some schools do teach children to join some, or all these letters. Check which handwriting style your child's school uses.

- Help and encourage your child to check their handwriting as they complete each activity.

- Discuss with your child what they have learnt.

- Let your child return to their favourite pages once they have been completed, to talk about the activities.

- Reward your child with plenty of praise and encouragement.

Special features

Yellow boxes: Introduce and outline the key handwriting ideas.

Published by Collins
An imprint of HarperCollinsPublishers Ltd
The News Building
1 London Bridge Street
London
SE1 9GF

Browse the complete Collins catalogue at
www.collins.co.uk

© HarperCollinsPublishers Ltd 2006
This edition © HarperCollinsPublishers Ltd 2015

10 9 8 7 6 5 4 3

ISBN 978-0-00-815145-4

British Library Cataloguing in Publication Data.

A Catalogue record for this publication is available from the British Library.

Design and layout by Graham M Brasnett and Contentra Technologies Ltd
Illustrated by Andy Tudor
Cover design by Sarah Duxbury and Paul Oates
Cover Illustration by Kathy Baxendale
Project managed by Sonia Dawkins

MIX
Paper from responsible sources
FSC™ C007454

Contents

Small letters

Trace and write.

a a a a   ·   ·   ·   ·   ·

c c c c   ·   ·   ·   ·   ·

e e e e   ·   ·   ·   ·

i i i i   ·   ·   ·   ·   ·

m m m m   ·   ·   ·

n n n n   ·   ·   ·   ·   ·

o o o   ·   ·   ·   ·   ·

r r r

s s s

u u u

v v v

w w w

x x x

z z z

Tall letters

Trace and write.

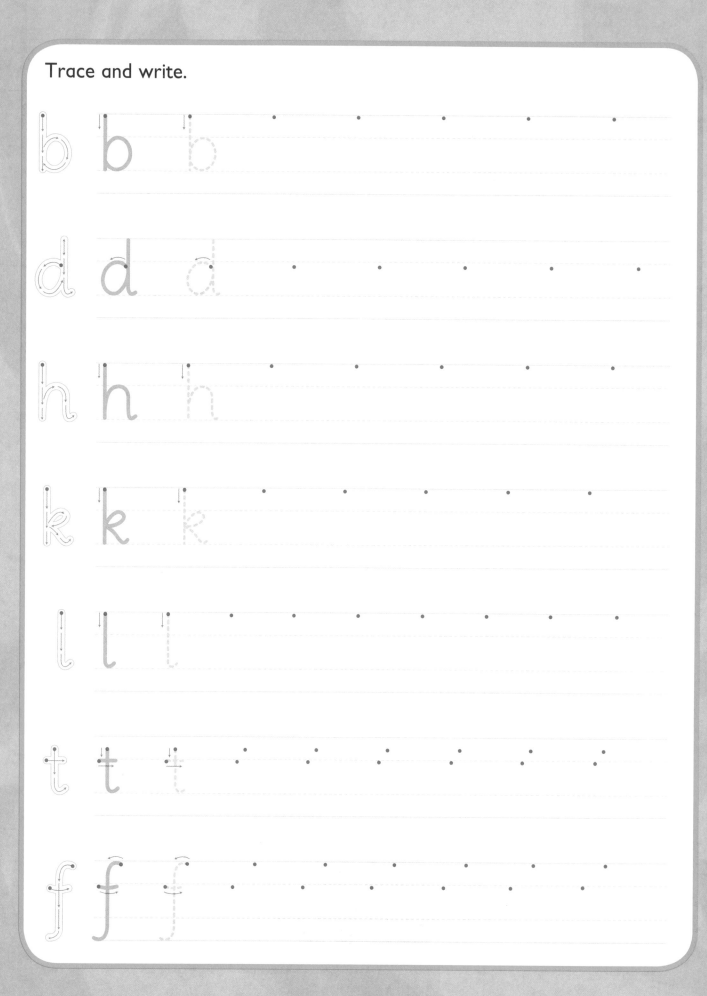

Descenders

Trace and write.

g g g

j j j

p p p

q q q

y y y

The first join

Trace the letters. Start at the red dot and follow the arrows.

Trace and write.

in   in   ·   ·   ·   ·

mp   mp   ·   ·   ·

ly   ly   ·   ·   ·   ·

tr   tr   ·   ·   ·   ·

dr   dr   ·   ·   ·

Trace and write.

 bin bin

 jam jam

pen pen

bun bun

zip zip

pin pin

yummy in my
tummy

yummy in my
tummy

9

The second join

Trace the letters. Start at the red dot and follow the arrows.

Trace and write.

it   it

al   al

nk   nk

lt   lt

cl   cl

Trace and write.

 ball ball

 hit hit

 bat bat

 bell bell

 hut hut

pull pull

I like the pink kite

I like the pink kite

The third join

Trace the letters. Start at the red dot and follow the arrows. Remember to go to the top of the letter o, stop, and back round to the left.

Trace and write.

do do . . .

ug ug . . .

ea ea . . .

ld ld . . .

nd nd . . .

Trace and write.

 bed bed

 cap cap

 bag bag

 cake cake

 hand hand

 banana banana

dad's mad if my
cat's bad

dad's mad if my
cat's bad

13

The fourth join

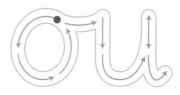

Trace the letters. Start at the red dot and follow the arrows.

Trace and write.

ou   ou   ·   ·   ·

ri   ri   ·   ·   ·   ·

vy   vy   ·   ·   ·

fr   fr   ·   ·   ·   ·

wi   wi   ·   ·   ·

Trace and write.

 wig wig

 boy boy

 one one

 ring ring

 home home

love love

a mouse in the house

a mouse in the house

15

The fifth join

Trace the letters. Start at the red dot and follow the arrows.

Trace and write.

ol   ol

of   of

rt   rt

fl   fl

ft   ft

Trace and write.

 owl owl

 hole hole

 knot knot

 book book

 whale whale

 school school

oh no, a mole in
a hole

oh no, a mole in
a hole

17

The sixth join

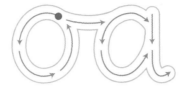

Trace the letters. Start at the red dot and follow the arrows. Remember to go to the top of the letter a, stop, and back round to the left.

Trace and write.

oa oa

vo vo

og og

ad ad

uc uc

Trace and write.

 dog dog

 frog frog

 wood wood

 door door

 sock sock

water water

a toad in the road
a toad in the road

ch and sh

These pairs of letters are often seen together at the beginning and end of words. Trace the letters.

Trace and write.

chair   child   arch

munch, crunch, chips for lunch

Trace and write.

shoe   shop   dish

splish, splash, the sheep had a wash

th and wh

These pairs of letters are often seen together at the beginning of words.
Th is also seen at the end of words too. Trace the letters.

Trace and write.

three   thumb   month

.   .   .

I think my brother has big teeth

Trace and write.

who   what   white

.   .   .

where, oh where, is my bear?

e, f and s

These three letters are tricky ones! Trace the letters. Now let's look at how they join to and from other letters.

Trace and write.

ee   *ee*   .   .   .   .

end   *end*   .   .   .   .   .

elephant   *elephant*   .

three   *three*   .   .   .

bears sleep easy
when it's breezy

Trace and write.

first first

after after

off off

the fly flew off
after the frog

Trace and write.

sun sun

crows crows

hiss hiss

scary snakes slide
and hiss

Break letters

These letters are break letters. We don't make a join after any of these letters.

b g j p q s x y z

Trace and write.

brother   brother

girl   girl

jump   jump

people   people

queen   queen

sock   sock

xylophone   xylophone

young   young

zebra   zebra

zebras jump over
purple boxes

Capital letters

Capital letters are similar to break letters. They don't join to any other letter.

Trace and write.

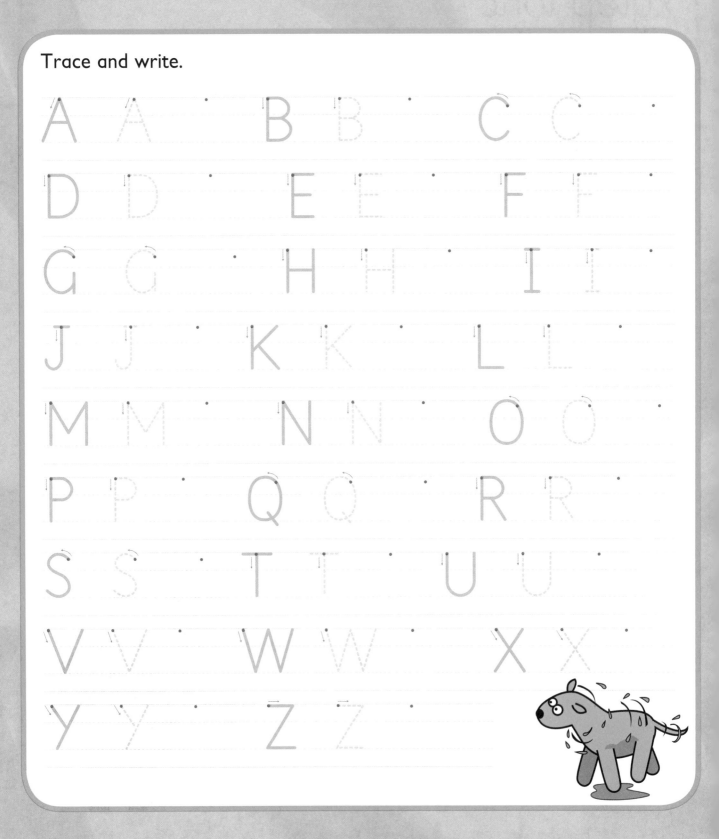

Days of the week

Trace and write.

Monday

Tuesday

Wednesday

Thursday

Friday

Saturday

Sunday

Numbers 1 to 20

Trace and write.

1   one

2   two

3   three

4   four

5   five

6   six

7   seven

8   eight

9   nine

10   ten

11   eleven

12   twelve

13   thirteen

14   fourteen

15   fifteen

16   sixteen

17   seventeen

18   eighteen

19   nineteen

20   twenty

Colours

Trace and write.

red

blue

green

yellow

pink

purple

orange

brown

white

Writing an invitation

In your best handwriting, write to a friend and invite them to your birthday party.

Dear _____

You are invited to
my birthday party

on _____

From _____

_____

Writing a letter

In your best handwriting, write a letter to thank someone in your family for a present. Put your address and the date at the top.

_____

_____

_____

_____

Dear_____

_____

_____

_____

_____

_____

_____

Love_____